BOA
EDITIONS LTD

The Dug-Up Gun Museum

o o o

The Dug-Up Gun Museum

Matt Donovan

o o o

AMERICAN CONTINUUM SERIES, NO. 197

BOA Editions, Ltd. ◦ Rochester, NY ◦ 2022

For information about permission to reuse any material from this book, please contact The Permissions Company at www.permissionscompany.com or e-mail permdude@gmail.com.

Publications by BOA Editions, Ltd.—a not-for-profit corporation under section 501 (c) (3) of the United States Internal Revenue Code—are made possible with funds from a variety of sources, including public funds from the Literature Program of the National Endowment for the Arts; the New York State Council on the Arts, a state agency; and the County of Monroe, NY. Private funding sources include the Max and Marian Farash Charitable Foundation; the Mary S. Mulligan Charitable Trust; the Rochester Area Community Foundation; the Ames-Amzalak Memorial Trust in memory of Henry Ames, Semon Amzalak, and Dan Amzalak; the LGBT Fund of Greater Rochester; and contributions from many individuals nationwide. See Colophon on page 94 for special individual acknowledgments.

Cover Design: Sandy Knight
Cover Art: Detail view of "Until" by Nick Cave
Interior Design and Composition: Michelle Dashevsky
BOA Logo: Mirko

BOA Editions books are available electronically through BookShare, an online distributor offering Large-Print, Braille, Multimedia Audio Book, and Dyslexic formats, as well as through e-readers that feature text to speech capabilities.

Cataloging-in-Publication Data is available from the Library of Congress.

BOA Editions, Ltd.
250 North Goodman Street, Suite 306
Rochester, NY 14607
www.boaeditions.org
A. Poulin, Jr., Founder (1938-1996)

CONTENTS

° ° °

∘ ∘ ∘

Portrait of America as a Friday the 13th Flashlight Tour of the Winchester Mystery House

It's easy to get lost in here. Folks go missing all the time.

Then we're down another corridor—*Keep moving,*

keep up, the guide tells us again—weaving our way to

the ballroom that inspired Disney's Haunted Mansion

with its parquet floor & ivy-laced words scrolling down

custom stained glass: *Wide unclasp the tables of their thoughts.*

Some believe, we learn, the widow used this space

to mourn & atone for her family's guns while others think

at each full moon she'd strike a chime & summon spirits

for a midnight feast. *This organ was donated to the house*

& it's hard to find a good organ donor. To complete the gag,

all we needed was a cued rimshot—*badum-ching*—piped in

above the sounds of rain & thunder playing throughout

the house on refrain before once again it's *watch-your-head-*

watch-your-step-here-we-go & we're off to the next room.

Who knows what lurks around each corner? the brochure asked, although a safe bet would be more bad puns, horror tropes,

history that doesn't add up. We've already wandered

the gift shop while waiting for our tour to begin, posed

with rifles for a keepsake photo in front of a green screen

that allowed us to appear in any of the rooms in the house.

We've wandered the Hall of Fires, seen a staircase disappear

into the ceiling, seen inch-deep kitchen cupboards, all of which

the grief-stricken heiress designed after being instructed

by a psychic to move west, the guide told us, & build a house

that would need to expand forevermore or else the victims

of her family's guns would seek revenge. Or something like that.

Out of remorse, fear, sidestepping blame, or some mishmash

of it all, the hammers could never stop. *Ask me anything, folks.*

If I don't know the answer, don't worry. I went to MSU—

"Make Stuff Up." We watch the beams of our souvenir flashlights

glide across ramshackle splendor & Tiffany windows

streaked by the real storm outside, too embarrassed to admit

we all expected more for our $49. *The House That Fear Built*

is dimly lit but not quite dark & bewildering enough to make our hearts pound. *Keep up. This is where we always lose people.*

In the séance room—*the labyrinth's heart,* with its false exits,

barred windows, blue trim—we're told Winchester would

enter this space, lock the doors, & reach out to the dead,

sometimes seeking forgiveness, sometimes asking

what to build next. A dramatic pause, & then at last

the ghost stories we've wanted to hear. One about a man

roaming the hallways. A doorknob rattling. A sound

like pounding, bursts of light. *These things happen*

all the time. And if in that moment none of us heard

how those tales of the dead echoed not the dead

but stories of our shootings & those who survived

(*A nearby bang. Someone gripping a shoulder. The sound*

of boots & breathing. Someone else in the room.) would you

blame us? That would entail stepping through aftermath

of a different kind, one a far cry from what we paid for.

On this unlucky night, our own muddled penance—as if

we'd ever use that word—is to keep moving. Up ahead,

the Door to Nowhere, which all of us needed to see.

o o o

Thousands or Millions of Tiny Dots of Varying Size

Once, I drove through Virginia slush to NRA Headquarters,

the winter air humming
                              with the emptiness of my plan
which was not more than the hope of doing something

beyond thoughts & prayers or any one word I might try

to use after seeing a self-defense catalog
with its photo of a young girl sitting cross-legged

against the cinder block grid of a school wall as she grips
a bulletproof backpack,
                              raising it up so that it conceals

her body more or less
                    behind a kid-friendly style,
which means blue with a cascade of emojis. For the last mile,

I stared at strip mall signs—Jenny Craig, Elegant Dancing,
Lead by Example Tae Kwon Do—that made me feel as if

I was lost in someone's idea of what America should be:

eye-catching, with plenty of parking & a flailing
inflatable tube man
                        who rises & falls, arms raised, frantic

to explain that a memory foam mattress sells for less guaranteed.

Without an appointment or idea
                              of what to do next,
I side-stepped the lobby's Tom Selleck cutout telling me

something about freedom
                              I forgot to write down & strolled into
the first room of the National Firearms Museum carrying

some vague hope of what? Whatever I'd come here to find,

it wasn't Annie Oakley's pistol or a custom 12-gauge
commemorating Princess Di's wedding or the gold inlaid

half-dozen geese soaring between
                              trigger & bolt
of a shotgun belonging to Hermann Göring. A few lines

of wall text described Bulino style, which meant, I learned,
the process of utilizing
                              thousands or millions of tiny dots

of varying size to create subtly shaded scenes, which ranged
from two coonhounds charging quail sheltered in long tangles

of grass, to a rifle's photorealistic Rolls Royce careening toward

a woman—topless, lips parted—nestled against a tiger.
And peering into one
                              mounted magnifying glass I saw

a gun engraved with a *Tribute to Picasso* featuring,
I swear, a miniature *Guernica* that mimicked each detail

of his horse & bull, the one jagged light & those bodies

we've seen so many times—
                              necks craned back, each mouth
in a wail—rendered in a way that reduced any trace

of sorrow to mere line & shape. America, I'm done

with prayers
         & mirrored vitrines, the yellow dots
of emojis wide-eyed on a kid's armored backpack

& black dots too numerous to count,
               spread across
those maps that track gun violence & for what? Then again,

here I am speaking to you within the silence of a poem

which is not much more than a form of prayer
we've heard too many times that makes

nothing change. By the time
            I'd finished wandering through
the other rooms, it was too late to do anything but drive

the same roads back to the hotel while half-listening
to classic rock & chasing after an idea about how we should

step back & see the shape made
            by those black dots scattered

across the US map,
         although haven't we done that already—
stepped back, & looked, & long known what we've made?

Shooting Justin Bieber & bin Laden in the Woods

It begins with rocks, leaves, hubcaps, a plastic bat

all tucked up where the sky should be
before the world is set right with an *Oops!*

& in one blurring swerve everything turns

right side up as a kid from behind the camera
proclaims what will be unleashed, namely

a can of paintball whoop-ass aimed at pictures
of Bieber & bin Laden duct-taped to buckets.

Someone called Usuck had decided my son needed
to see what was about to go down. This was back when

we monitored his texts, thinking we could save him
from who-knows-what while also wondering if we needed

to protect the world from whatever he might hurl forth
from his phone, which most of the time was acronyms

traded in rapid-fire bursts mixed with that laughing-but-crying

emoji, the one with two oversized teardrops sprouting
like a pair of blue tusks from an eyes-scrunched-shut face.

There was no need to watch what Usuck sent
all the way through, although I wanted to see

what would happen at the end, which turned out to be
what was promised: the sound of shots

at first beginning with a steady beat before becoming
a drum roll for paint-splatter, *hell-yeahs,*

the smirk or glower on faces reduced to shreds,

two spinning buckets & then a kid running to see
close-up what he'd done. Usuck & panting, grinning kid,

there's a light snow coming down just now
& because the wide, blank face of our neighbor's house

is filled with the wavering light of whatever
they too have chosen to watch, I wouldn't mind asking you

about the pleasures of the trigger, about the sky

that somehow doesn't cast down upon us
what we've shot & left behind—plywood, bottles,

what looks like a rowing machine & any other targets
roped to a low-hanging branch that help stop

rage from becoming grief. Then again, what use

is the conceit of a conversation that will never take place
when there are so many things online cued & ready

to play? Up next: *What happens*

to a Hand Grenade in a Microwave? Up next:
Watermelon vs. Artillery Shells. Up next:

Company Offers Reenactment of bin Laden Raid,
where each night participants arrive in Pakistan—

played by an office building in Minneapolis—
where they storm rooms clutching guns, weaving

through metal chairs & self-defense dummies
before, without warning, they become

as ready as they'll ever be. You'll need to take him out.
I don't want to write a letter to your parents.

No one wants to write that letter. We'd all rather watch

someone ill-trained burst through a door to find
the man who had been promised,

sitting on a mattress, wearing eye protection & a fake beard
that resembles a fistful of wheat, raising a fake gun

slowly enough to be shot by military-grade simulation rounds
before slumping to the floor & trying his best

to still his breath. Mission as always accomplished.

Instead of this, I should be watching the snow
continue its slow work erasing our world,

or even a video I wish I could see that would be nothing

but a never-veering shot of the same man
bored in a costume turban, alone in a room

& thinking who-knows-what as he traces
the long loops of the stitching in a sky-blue quilt

& the door for once never opens. Up next:

Hendrix Makes His Guitar Into a Machine Gun just after
the rocket's red glare, when he gives up on melody

& wrenches his Woodstock solo into gunfire, explosions,
a long shriek of feedback followed by the opening notes

of *Taps*. Up next: *Is a Fish Tank Bulletproof?*
As always, the answer is *no*, this time

in the form of glinting water perched on a milk crate
that becomes the shattered thing

we knew it would be before it's all rewound—
slosh of water rushing backward, broken glass

slipping into place—only to explode again
in slow-mo for our pleasure. If you watch

the mock-raid video all the way to the end,
someone asks bin Laden what it's like to be shot

night after night & the guy says *warm*.

The Wrong Question More Than Once

For most of the shift, it was more about not looking
bored or wanting to seem invisible behind the ER desk
while nothing much happened at all. A Cubs banner
twitched in the air vent. A nurse wearing a "Welcome
to the Madhouse" T-shirt described a stick-figure meme.
Someone wanted to know why a drunken John Doe
had pissed in the supply closet & a man half-hidden
behind a triage curtain never stopped staring me down.
Off-rhythm pings from somewhere chased a pulsing
beep that made it seem as if something had gone wrong.
I asked & then later asked again: nothing was ever wrong.
And because the shift would be ending soon, I asked
the question I was there to ask after reading about
a surgeon who'd claimed our gun problems could be
solved if only we'd release the autopsy photos
from Sandy Hook. *That's the only chance*, she insisted,
for this to ever be reversed. No doubt even if I'd found
a better shape to my words, the doctor chaperoning
my visit would have given me the same look that said
as an act of mercy to everyone within earshot, please
shut the fuck up. The idea seemed stolen from
Scared Straight, he said, the 1970s documentary in which
prison lifers rage at juvenile delinquents as a means
of mending lives. Shoes squeaked. Phones rang.
More off-rhythm pings. *Besides, why would seeing
bodies with gunshot trauma make any difference
to Second Amendment fans? They'd say 'Yeah,
that's what guns do.'*
        The next day in the basement
of Saint Sabina church, talking to the woman
from Purpose Over Pain, what easier way to proclaim
what little I knew than to ask the same question
even after she told me—calmly, quietly—how her son
was shot unloading a drum kit outside a church?

We have mass shootings all the time in Chicago
& they do nothing. It's a problem when it's white lives,
but when a six-year-old gets shot on the south side,
it's just crime as usual. And after she walked me
upstairs through the pews, past the sculpture
of an ash-gray figure gripping a pistol with one hand
while piercing the chest of a young girl with another,
leading me through the locked front doors & out
to the display case lining the sidewalk—was I thinking
even then about how photos of the dead might
enact change? *This is our memorial wall*, she told me,
matter-of-fact. *I knew everyone here.* She watched me
for a moment scanning the faces stapled in place—
school photos, caps & gowns, plenty of thumbs-ups
& basketballs, children a few months old—before
pointing at a teenager grinning in a white tuxedo
in front of a painted backdrop of a skyline & fountain.
There's my Terrell right there.

Planet Fitness

I'm watching the police shoot an unarmed Black man while I run on a treadmill. His arms are raised and he's walking backward toward his car as I run in place and an officer aims a gun and others arrive on the scene. The man's hands are empty when he falls against his car and they're empty when he drops to the ground. From the viewpoint of the helicopter hovering above, Terence Crutcher—his name, I'll later learn, after looking it up, since no one said it as the footage played— walks backward, then dies on continuous loop on four of the fourteen screens. There's Terence Crutcher on the ground once more. There are his hands raised. There's his car, stopped in the middle of the road. There's the guardrail, ditch. Here's the moment—it's becoming familiar already—when the helicopter swings to one side and the view becomes partially blocked before Terence Crutcher drops from sight and then he's on the ground. Now the footage begins to play on a split screen—there's the backward walk, his empty hands raised, the circling as he falls to the road—but his death is already a bit smaller because people have begun to speak. I can't hear what they're saying, but I watch their mouths move across from where Terence Crutcher lies in the road. Behind the row of TVs, in bright gold on the wall, a gigantic thumb's-up crashes through a cogged wheel next to emblazoned slogans. *No Critics. Judgment Free Zone.* Someone out there wants me to feel comfortable. Someone wants me to feel good. On other days when I'm running, I'll anchor my eyes on that gigantic thumb or perhaps stare directly into one of the O's in the words *You Belong!* but today, instead, I'm watching Terence Crutcher stand in the road with his arms raised. The sound is off, but captions appear in boxes at the bottom of the screens. *That looks like a bad dude*, someone says from the helicopter hovering above, and then, just after the shots are fired, *They're going to need to get this eastbound closed down.* The words lag then lurch forward again each time someone speaks. A day or two from now, I'll learn that Terence Crutcher was born three minutes before his twin sister, that he loved the Dallas Cowboys and the gospel song "I Won't Complain," that he left behind three teenage daughters and a four-year-old son, but none of that fills the boxes on the screens. I'm running in place as Terence Crutcher walks backward or raises his hands or dies next to his car once more and whatever was said is being said yet again out of sync in a box of words.

Here the Thing with Feathers Isn't Hope

but a 400-pound pistol in the bed
of a pickup, welded together from
scrapyard metal & stamped with names
of kids shot & killed near the artist's home.
Except for all the feathers, dyed
cotton-candy blue & affixed to the pistol's
cylinder & grip, wrapping the length
of the barrel with a flourish like a boa
entwining a neck, it might seem like
any other oversized gun. *Conversation
Piece*, he called it, although the feathers
came later, only after he'd begun driving
south with a plan to haul the sculpture
from Chicago to Atlanta, then back
through Charleston & Sandy Hook.
But when he stopped for gas the first time,
he knew his art had failed when a man
sprinted across the parking lot to say
Goddamn, that's one bad ass gun.
Something needed to change. Maybe
feathers could turn the pistol into
a thing you approached with a question
instead of praise. And if the plumes
now covered some of the names, burying
the elegies hammered into metal,
what choice did he have but to continue
driving through town after town, listening
to the wind's song whipping across
the wide mouth of the barrel, tending
to the gun now & then from a sack
of feathers he kept in the back seat to use
whenever storms lashed things loose?

Solipsism: A Story

Victim mentality, he told me, *means sitting with your back to the door*
        anywhere at all, even—I was learning—while sipping a Red Bull

& surrounded by tourists at the hotel Buffalo Bill named after his daughter.
        I'd more likely leave my house without my pants than without my gun.

So even though we were talking in the Irma's side saloon about plans
        to arm Cody's teachers—scenario training, lockable holsters, the deterrence

of not knowing who's armed—the theme was readiness is all. Pistol in hand
        when opening the front door. Peering through his gun shop's window

before stepping inside. And how whenever he drives to another town,
        he'll have an AR-15 & extra mags in a quick zip-off on the back seat,

a .45 on the hip & ankle gun strapped tight, while his girlfriend rides shotgun
        with a .38 in her purse & a .40 caliber in the back without fail. Five guns

for a drive to Billings: *Just in case, you never know*. What else could I think
        but you have to be shitting me & I can't wait to tell this tale. Before

leaving town, I circled back to his store, wanting to hard-grip his hand,
        see what else he might let slip. As I strolled the rifles & pistols,

clips & cases, gun safes & gun powder, waiting for him to finish
        whatever he was doing with the gun he held, the green eyes

of a taxidermized leopard stared at something that was not me,
        its dark mouth hinged open enough to show the curved shape

someone had chosen for its tongue. *Hey, I'm glad you came back.*
        Don't take this the wrong way, but I've been telling folks I met some guy

who doesn't own a gun, an unarmed dad, & no one can believe it.
        We looked at each other for a half-beat, maybe more, & didn't say

what we were thinking about how each of us had chosen to move through this world,
        or how both of us by then had turned into a story about something impossible

glimpsed somewhere we thought we knew. I haven't spoken to him since.

D-Day: Albrightsville, Pennsylvania

The invasion was imminent and—jam-packed into a makeshift landing craft, sandwiched between seasoned soldiers and greenhorn rookies, between Red Sox caps and helmets adorned with fangs—we knew we were about to die.

My boat's crew included Sideshow, sporting a camouflaged kilt, and Harley Quinn, Batman's sexpot villain, decked out in pigtails and purple spandex. Near a band of amiable Canadians, one guy had shown up for battle wearing only sneakers and a pair of shorts. Tattooed on the bicep in front of me: a bald eagle, the Statue of Liberty, exploding fireworks, and the words *We the People* bursting into flame on star-spangled, jigsaw-like shapes.

We knew what was out there on the far side of the shore. Beyond the waves—which were not waves at all, but trampled grass cluttered with shipping containers, lengths of sewer pipe, a wooden helicopter, and girders bolted into mine-like shapes— hundreds of Germans lurked in the hemlocks.

Beyond the first row of trees, acres of stand-in French countryside held yet more Nazis, stashes of Enola Gay-brand smoke grenades, a Mazda truck converted into a tank from archived German blueprints. There were pieces of wood painted with amateur renderings of looted art (Van Gogh's *Almond Blossoms*; Munch's *Scream*), and propane tanks labeled *Mustard Gas* that, if captured, would earn you extra points.

We were breathing heavily and sweating inside our protective masks. At noon, the doors of the Utah, Omaha, Gold, Juno, and Sword would drop and the shooting would begin. Despite the looming slaughter, the soldiers were keen for battle. Some were kitted out in shaggy military-grade ghillie suits while others embraced non-regulation options: Gumby wielding a studded hammer, a unicorn with a hot pink tail, an evil clown, a full-body foam-rubber penis.

There were nearly fifty of us loaded into the Utah and we'd been stewing side by side for an hour. I was there to observe, hoping to talk proxy guns, as well as what it meant to enlist into battle as a Nazi. No one in my landlocked vessel was having it. Some of the soldiers began singing maritime-themed songs, launching into a round of "Row row row your boat" that devolved into the seventies pop hit "Rock the Boat."

The night before, Skirmish Paintball had hosted its annual diplomatic reception. This gathering of top brass was really just a tongue-in-cheek get-together beneath a wooden pavilion, an excuse for old friends to raise plastic cups of champagne. Reunited combatants hugged, fist-bumped, took turns smacking each other on the ass with a baguette. Several times someone climbed atop a picnic table and delivered a mock Third Reich salute.

It's just a game, I was told by many players fighting on the side of the Nazis. *It's so much better to begin the battle in the shade*, a US Army vet said, referring to how the Allies are packed into boats beneath a blazing sun whereas the Germans take up positions in the delicious cool of the woods.

It's more about physiological hunter-aggressor needs than any one war, the owner of Skirmish said. Besides, swastikas had been banned from the event a few years earlier. And yet, participants strutted about in full-length leather SS jackets. One team fighting for the German side had angled an RV so that their swastika flag wasn't visible from the road. One buzz-cut player who hurried past me in a field had scrawled a swastika in blue ballpoint on his neck.

Each year, nearly five thousand people enlist for this D-Day event. Over the course of the weekend, organizers claimed, more than ten million paintball rounds would be fired, with the heaviest artillery bombardment taking place during the first invasion. *When the battle begins, the sky above will darken with paintballs*, I'd been told in those exact words more than once.

Two Skirmish referees pressed their backs against our boat's drop-door as a means of sealing us in. Fantom, the Utah's commander, began the same speech he delivers each year. Amid the rising chants of *U-S-A*, Fantom wanted us to know a few things.

I'm tasked with the defense of Utah Beach. It takes a whole lot of guts, and a whole lot of man, to move out of these boats, and you're probably going to die. This is just paintball, and we're just out here to have a good time. But if you can summon even a tenth of the guts of the men who fought in this war, then it doesn't matter how many Germans attack—you will hold the line! Harley Quinn shouted back *Hell, yeah!*

Even though it was still a few minutes before noon, the Germans opened fire. Paint capsules exploded against the Utah's frame, and the referees raised their protective shields in anticipation of what was to come.

Second Rangers! Fantom yelled. *When I say, "Kill who?" you say "Kill them!"* This call-and-response continued for a while. Two men near the front of the boat lobbed a few grenades, and wisps of celery-colored smoke clouded the battlefield. *It's going to be beautiful!* Fantom called out. At high noon, a siren wailed and the door of the Utah dropped. Someone hollered *Here we go!* and everyone dashed forward with a whoop.

Land of 1000 Dances

Here we go again: a room

crammed with portraits gives way
to embroidered lines meant to be branches

of the Charter Oak—where, legend has it,
someone once hid a declaration of freedom

in the hollow of its trunk—which leads to
a hodgepodge of chrome behind glass—

clocks, hair dryers, toasters, a lunchbox—
that gives way to a room

crowded with the Colt Firearms Collection.
Have you ever wanted to move through

a different world altogether, one in which you might
kill some time on a whim at a museum without

being blindsided by yet more guns

before Patti Smith takes the stage down the block?
Stuck in traffic on the drive to Hartford,

I heard the original *Land of 1000 Dances*,
a song that doesn't begin with the familiar plunge into

naming all the ways our bodies can shudder—

the pony, the alligator, the mashed potato—
but instead offers two lines of a capella gospel.

Children, go where I send you.
I'm gon' send you to that land.

A few weeks ago, after locking the door,
lowering blinds, turning out the lights,

my son's first-grade teacher pressed a finger to her lips,
then made the class crouch in a back corner

as the nurse prowled the hall, rattling handles,
pounding doors, trying to lure the kids out, calling

each of their names. Although
no one likes this drill, the principal explained,

it's a price for freedom we can't afford
to lose. It secures a liberty that began

in the dark space of a tree
toppled long ago. *The Charter Oak is Prostrate* blares

a headline above what seems like an obituary
that can't decide whether to blame the inevitable

corrosion of time or the violence
of a single storm for uprooting the beloved tree.

Either way, dirges played, bells tolled, & when
the crowd gathered, *manly eyes were nourished,*

the news clippings tell us, meaning tears fell
in the aftermath of the unthinkable.

Is anything unthinkable anymore? Last night,
a woman returned to a playground

& shot the man who'd scolded her son, which is one story
among thousands I could choose. When no one knew

what words should come next,

Frankie "Cannibal" Garcia on the spot filled the space
with its hook—*NA na na na NA*—

that now we can't imagine
the song without. Someone might holler

Shall not be infringed. Someone might believe
a revolver fitted with a grip that was carved

from the Charter Oak is like hammering
ploughshares into swords. *NA na na na NA.*

What if I tried to twist my way to Colt's watercolors
on a framed patent for a new cylinder,

with its circle of dark circles within a circle

the color of the sea except for
a center space left blank that serves as the hub

for what he knew would allow everything to move
without fail, letting bullets give way easily

to bullets, each chamber slipping
perfectly into place, all of which sounds like

an American vision of heaven:

no surprises, absolute efficiency, a profit margin
widened even more. It wasn't always like this.

For years, Colt flailed with pepperbox designs,
misfires, unreliable pins. One critic wrote that each time

someone fired a Colt,
one could *observe the escape*

of lateral flame like the halo around the head of a saint.
These days, no one worries much

about halos, & if I believe the writing on the wall
of this room, Colt's guns have become

as dependable as the mottled gold statue
on display that looms beneath a painted dome of sky,

both of which replicate
the starry blue-zinc cupola & reared-back

horse once mounted on the factory's roof
that comes to us from a legend

about a saddle-flung man saved
after his horse shattered the attacker's spear.

Just now, I'm thinking less about
the heraldic than the story of Colt's widow

one night watching a fire in the factory grow
until all of it—stars, horse, the roof above

the world she knew—plummeted

into flames, collapsing into the machines below
that lathe, jig, cut grooves. No one knows

where this statue came from, but here it is,
reared back above us, its teeth still seizing

the weapon, as if intent on saving someone

from a battle that took place in a legend
centuries ago. *Rampant*, from the French,

meaning *fierce*, meaning *ravenous*

as the horses from that Patti Smith song. Remember?
The one that begins with a boy attacking

another boy in a hall which gives way
to a vision of horses in flames, pouring in

from all sides, which gives way to a voice

telling us again about the twist, the pony,
& all the other verbs that inhabit this *Land*

of 1000 Dances & asking if we like it like that.

○ ○ ○

Portrait of America as the Hands of Peter Graves in *The Night of the Hunter*

Did you think I meant the knuckles of Robert Mitchum's

Preacher spelling out *Hate & Love*? But who needs

more abstraction & pantomimes of justice, which is all

the Preacher's selling at the diner as he rehashes

that back-and-forth tussle between his own hands.

No matter what words are inscribed on skin, no matter

the moral about Hate being *down for the count*,

we know those same hands will unfold & do whatever

the Preacher wants to do. *What have I to fear*,

he'll sing as a silhouette gliding along the horizon,

his voice carrying across every hill, *leaning*

on the everlasting arms? There was a time when

all I'd wanted to ask about *The Night of the Hunter*

had to do with the scene when the camera turns from

the sway of underwater reeds & lingers on the body

of the Preacher's wife, strapped into her car in a white dress

with her throat slit & hair alive in the water's current.

What makes that moment the most beautiful image

ever made now seems like a question I might have asked

at a different time, in a different country, where

the river doesn't lead downstream, as it does

in the film, to a canopy of night that somehow

resembles both a star-filled sky &, in the same breath,

a black cloth riddled with holes. Look, instead,

at the earlier scene where Peter Graves careens

home after robbing a bank. Seconds later, the police

turn up, yet give him all the time he needs to choose

where he'll stash the loot before kneeling in the grass

& talking to his son about promises. When the shot

cuts to a view through the cruiser's windshield,

one cop says, almost a little bored, as if watching

from a great distance, *That's him*, & the other replies

He's probably still got that gun. There's no doubt

he still holds the gun as he strolls his yard before

disappearing to find a needle & thread to stitch

together his daughter's doll after tucking the cash inside.

When the other policemen arrive on the scene

& close in beneath the long shadows of the pines,

still offering all the time in the world, they make

the shape of one small curve in what seems to be

a different kind of river that spilled from its banks

long ago, one beneath the surface of which

you can look & see what happened in Martinsburg,

just across the state from where the movie was filmed,

when a policeman approached a Black man & asked

why he was walking in the street. The blank gaze

of the dash-cam offers us not much more than a curb,

some parking meters, a blurry blaze of light where

South Queen Street ends as we hear the man, whom

the police will learn is named Wayne Jones only after

he's dead, explain he's *trying to get to a distance.*

Can I get there? he asks. The answer, the cop decides,

means telling Wayne Jones what to do with his hands

& then, between calls for backup, where his hands

need to be five more times. After Wayne Jones flees

from a scene he didn't understand, the police form

a semicircle &, within seconds, from only a few feet away,

shoot him twenty-two times. Any answer to any question

you might want to ask wouldn't begin to plumb

the depths of this river that's not a river yet something

that won't stop flowing nonetheless. Although a judge

proclaimed some things—*homicide, excessive*—none of them

proved indelible & these words too will tumble down the page

before they disappear & yet here I am still rummaging

the past, returning even to this film with its world of white

picket fences in which Peter Graves has time to explain

to his son that the word *promise* means *forever*

as the police give him time to say goodbye there

in the sunlight of his yard as he holds the pistol

with one hand & grips his son with the other & we can

watch as he surrenders into their arms through

a backward glide that seems like a kind of dance

or as if they're acting out the words of a hymn

about someone being carried into the distance.

o o o

Jack Ruby's .38 Colt Cobra

Because even after you put death aside—keeping in your sights not Oswald's ruptured gut, but the very idea of the gun beginning to grow, becoming a new kind of try-me, a sure bet that Ruby could grip, strap to his thigh, flaunt to protect the earnings of his half-assed strippers, ventriloquist acts, and hustled bottles of rotgut champagne, and how, after he had a buddy cop score it from Ray's (*bada boom*, saving him eighteen bucks), the Colt bloomed from a theory of backup to an actual sweet heft in his hands; or how, on that particular day, after he parked the Olds and cooed a goodbye to Sheba, his dachshund, his sugar, his baby, he was perhaps thinking less about the wad of cash than words like *hero, wrist-slap, crown* as he strode down the parking lot ramp off Main, then mingled incognito with the press, ready to gawk at the man who shot JFK, but also beginning to feel that tug on his sleeve, beginning to realize he could wring some use from his grief after all, unlike everyone else at home "glued to the tube," as we'd later say, hoping to glimpse a few handcuffed steps, not knowing they were moments away from watching the first-ever broadcast death, which truth be told was not much more than a procession of Stetsons, white shirts, and ties that became an arm-cocked lunge and a one-off *bang* followed by the camera herky-jerky showing Oswald disappearing into a sea of suits; or how it would take the next day's freeze-framed money shot to let the moment chime beyond that first fleeting shock, beyond the image we've seen and seen again, where Oswald's lips are forever locked on that lopsided O that tells us precisely nothing about death or what it means to have a bullet burrow into the lower lateral chest wall at the exact moment the shutter is clicked by Robert Jackson, the man who began banking on the Pulitzer even as the image first swam into view in its chemical bath, forever turning what had already been printed by the rival *Dallas Morning News* into a mere snapshot, a near-miss, an also-there, given how the payoff we crave was still in the split-second offing; or how the gun, decades later, let loose from the courts at last, was auctioned to Anthony Pugliese III, who first fingered his $220,000 prize through a Crown Royal sack passed to him beneath a table in Little Italy; or how the murder weapon became, for Pugliese, a notch in the belt, a trophy, a claim, one more bit of memorabilia he owned, along with Indiana Jones's prop bullwhip and the hat worn by the dissolving wicked witch during *Oz's what-a-world-what-a-world* scene; or how the gun became something of a celebrity, appearing on *Larry King Live* like some come-back actor hawking a new book; or, even more, how the Colt became a money-making machine, given how Pugliese would shoot it into his swimming pool, then gather the deep-end bounty and mount each bullet in a frame along with an 8 x 10 of Oswald's assassination, signed by two of the escorting detectives and accompanied by a decree that confirmed it was indeed a relic from *The Most Famous Gun in the World*; or how, years later, Jack's brother Earl agreed to squeeze off some rounds from the legendary gun (*maybe 63 times?* Pugliese joked), this time into a barrel brimming with hose water because *why not* and, besides, Earl's bankable Ruby DNA could reap a few bucks more from each framed-bullet sale; or how the gun for years was left more or less forgotten in a bank vault after its owner became entrenched in a plan to convert 27,000 acres of Florida real estate near Yeehaw Junction into *Destiny*, an eco-friendly housing development with its *Come to Your Destiny* slogan and intravenous vitamin injections and planned kibosh on anything but organic food, a place *where kids can ride their bikes down the sidewalks and people can sit out on their front porch*, all of which unraveled after Pugliese was accused of defrauding his partner, a co-founder of Subway sandwiches, of just over a million bucks, then funneling the cash for personal use, including an $11,000 moat-chiller, which is, it turns out, exactly what the name implies: a device that chills the moat around one's home—what do you make of America then?

Yeats Claimed a Poem Should Come Together

with a click like a box shutting its lid, yet
given what's for sale in the Battlefield Vegas

gift shop, would it be better to choose
the shotgun shells glued together to form a cross

or that pink hoodie with the word *LOVE* spelled out
using a Glock, a hand grenade, a switchblade,

& the long dark shape of an AR-15 in order
to suggest something closing?

Operation Lion Claws: Fort Hood, Texas

After Red Hawk One announced it was time to lock and load, it was all gunfire and grenade blasts, moving out and hustling like hell, securing perimeters and scrambling into bushes, jabbing my imitation rifle into empty cinder block rooms and hollering *Clear!* with as much conviction as I could muster.

It was about men dressed in regulation camouflage, holstering fake pistols, slipping on balaclavas, filling canteens, and stuffing backpacks with proxy grenades. It was about imitation long range rifles, mortar launchers, wide-barreled revolvers, AK-47s, and machine guns dangling chains of fake bullets. Some of the patches on uniforms proclaimed code names: Raptor, Crazyhorse, Jack Frost, Drago. Some depicted a cross bookended by two rifles that hovered above the words *Waterboarding is how we baptize the terrorists.*

It was about following the rules: *Call your hits. Use your dead rag. Shoot semi-auto whenever indoors. If you hear "Blind Man," someone's real world hurt and you need to immediately cease fire.* Per the Geneva Conventions, we weren't permitted to shoot civilians—bussed-in Phi Kappa Sigma frat brothers dressed in headscarves and robes—although we could attempt to bribe them with Skittles for intel. *And be a good sport.*

It was about being shoved through the door of a mosque-shaped building during a raid that began with our commander saying *Let's take this bitch before lunch* and ended with all of us mowed down and someone wailing *Mommy!* to much laughter.

It was about learning that dying offers reprieve. Sometimes, I hoped to be shot in order to put down my weapon and lie there in the fields, bleeding out beneath an enormous Texas sky. Sometimes, I milled about at the Respawn location in order to listen to the dead swap stories. Someone had plowed through a backdoor. Someone had held that motherfucking roof. Someone had fought in crazy-ass tunnels they'd found beneath the embassy, but that asshole hadn't called his hit. Someone had been shot in the kisser at two hundred feet and now was missing a front tooth.

The game was airsoft, meaning fake guns that fire plastic BBs. But the real game was verisimilitude, one-to-one gun proxies, pushing past approximation, suspending disbelief.

Our battle was sponsored by Operation Lion Claws, one of many companies that offer simulated war experiences. You could choose, for instance, to rack up kills in a bamboo jungle at the Sanna Movie Ranch or experience urban combat modeled on the Battle of Mogadishu (a.k.a. Black Hawk Down) at the remains of the Packard Automotive Plant in Detroit.

Or, like me, after being told that mere observers of these simulations are not permitted on federal military bases, you could instead choose to register for the weekend battle and pretend to wage fake war at a real-world training facility. The premise—does it even matter?—involves Russia trying to wrest control of such-and-such region. *The stakes are real. Our points will be tallied at the end.*

It is well that war is so terrible, Robert E. Lee once wrote. *Otherwise we should grow too fond of it.*

By nightfall, the war with Russia had paused. You could hit the tents, crack a beer, get some rest before war resumed the next day. Or you could up the ante with that evening's Tier One event. *You won't be disappointed. Things are going to be lit up. You're breeching doors, you're getting your hands bloody. It's like the Navy Seal raid on bin Laden's compound. Only a few slots remain.* I handed over my debit card and paid the additional fee.

This situation was urgent. We needed to kill or capture an Islamic militant. We needed to cross the border, raid enemy camps, contend with crooked cops. We needed to take a whirlybird to the drop site, gather evidence, stick together, not fail.

Make this as realistic as you want. The amount of stress that you put on yourself and your battle buddies is up to y'all. If you're shot, hit the floor and die in a way that will make your buddies go, "Oh shit, Dallas got hit. Dallas is on the floor." It's all about integrity, guys.

Our commander had begun telling us how this mission couldn't afford any lone-wolf soldiers when he stopped and jabbed a finger into the air. *Look at that—aerial gunnery, guys!* We whipped around and saw army tracer rounds being fired from the dark shadow of a helicopter hovering a few miles away. Bright red streaks flared through the sky. Someone clenched their fist in the air and made little *pew-pew* sounds.

We clambered onto the bed of the pickup (our helicopter stand-in), tucked our rifles between our knees, and roared off through the night. If someone switched out our airsoft weapons for cap guns and instated an earlier bedtime, there wouldn't be much difference between our troop's imaginary bang-bang action and the war games we played as kids when we'd besiege our cul-de-sac, stalking and taking aim at each other as popsicle-sticky soldiers.

Shouts in the distance, gunfire, an explosion. *Go loud!* someone yelled, which meant bomb blasts and glow-in-the-dark BBs streaking the air and a lot of other people yelling *Roger that* and *We've got a man down* as the enemy raced past, screaming *Allahu Akbar* and firing potshots at the soldiers inside the buildings.

We needed to move out and lay down cover. We needed to get next door and sweep some rooms. We had to split up but stay on mission. Soon enough, I was killed and thought I needed to head to the Respawn location, but the commander set me straight. *Remember, when you die, you come to me*, he said, then made a low hum and a hocus-pocus gesture with his hands. *You're alive*, he proclaimed. *Your soul is back.*

My soul was returned in time for me to climb into the back of our helicopter-truck and head back down the road to base. Although we'd failed to extract the target, we'd escaped with evidence bags containing computer hard drives, relay switches, cell phones, and uranyl nitrate. *That was outfuckingstanding. Pure textbook, I shit you not. You all highly earned your Tier One patches.*

Low clouds hung thick and gray when the war wrapped up the next morning. The soldiers returned to base camp grinning and caked with grime. There was talk of prizes and a swag giveaway, and folks began unfolding lawn chairs in anticipation of that morning's raffle. We gathered around a flatbed cart affixed with a small white flag featuring a single black star, a drawing of what looked like a torpedo, and the words *Come and take it.*

On the T-shirt in front of me, running from muzzle to stock along a rifle's black shape: *Make no mistake, I will defend my family, I will defend the weak, I will defend our way of life. I will bring the fight to your home to keep you out of mine.*

An Operation Lion Claws administrator stood on the bed of a pickup with his hands on his hips and ended the suspense at last. For those of you keeping track, America won.

Green Means Literally a Thousand Things or More

So concludes an essay on "Fern Hill," in which the student seems
somewhere between jazzed up & pissed off that green might mean
so many things from one stanza to the next: here, a blooming

Eden proxy; here, rot made by the grip of time. For starters. Or
that sun-slaked field, not far from our classroom, as lush-green
as any Welsh farmyard, grayed overnight with frost. Emerald

beer bottle hurled from a car. The slack-jawed lime-green
goblin face spanning a front porch post-Halloween
for so many weeks it looks like it's here to stay. The long-ago

brown-green of Cleveland, where it rained always & without pity
upon a past I crave despite myself & our team lost always 14 – 2.
Every time we waited in the bleachers for the game to resume,

my father would look down upon the outfield's mowed lines
& proclaim *Still a lot of green out there*, meaning anything
can happen & will. Have you ever heard in a crowd the saddest part

of "Take Me Out to the Ballgame," where everyone lies & pretends
we don't care if we ever get back & makes the last word echo
twice more? We always want to get back, whether or not

we're hailing childhood green. Like the student in her essay,
I too could keep rattling off images of spring & decay—June
sunset horizon flash, summer hair stained olive from churning

over-chlorinated pools, green shadow of a hand that makes it feel,
as it says in the poem, as if owls were bearing everything away—
instead of looking again at the image online I glimpsed before

returning to my still-ungraded hay-high stack of student work.
Maybe you saw it too? Maybe you also had the spellbound luck
of wandering to other tasks instead of asking what it means to know

anything can happen in a wholly different way, instead of looking
once more at the slash of police tape that is the only horizon
that matters just now for the two men in the photograph who sit

together on the curb, faces glowing blue-red in the lights, both of them
bleary-eyed but alive, swaddled in aftermath & a blanket that is green,
a detail that couldn't matter less, given how the numbers of the dead

still rise. Here we are again, as inevitable as the clock's tick, looking in
at a place that now will never be young again. Is there a way to say it—
There's been a shooting—that will allow it to be heard, remembered

& heard, without the easy glide of our past tense? That will stop us
from wanting to turn to anything under the wide starry sky that is not
the green fire burning in the minds of those men or the green

of a blanket America provides & provides without change?

Mass Shootings Are Actually Pretty Rare, but Here's What to Do If You're Ever in One

— After Self Magazine *& Wisława Szymborska*

It could happen. Once it happens.
Earlier, later. Closer today but not to you. You'll survive

because you ran, because you hid.
Because you were first. Because last.
Because alone. Because the others.

Of course, highly unlikely.
Of course, situationally aware.
Be sure the door won't open.
Be sure the door won't close.
Conceal. Barricade.
To the left, the right. Accept the sound
for what it is.

If you're lucky, there will be a fence.
If you're lucky, the fence has been removed.
Perhaps a mug of coffee, door wedge, scissors,
the broken leg of a chair. A turn, a shirt, a second.
Perhaps a ball point pen.

Thanks to calm, an element of surprise. In spite of,
& yet. What would happen if the eyes, the throat,
the knees, a step away?

So he is here? Straight from the moment
without end? The net, the gun? But you, the mesh?
I can't be silent enough.
Listen,
how quickly your heart is beating & mine.

Guy with a Gun

There's the phrase once again—*The only thing that stops a bad guy with a gun*—this time pasted on a Subaru's fender, its rote answer tagging along in a faded Wild West font. Today, though, idling in traffic, instead of knee-jerk counterarguments and a few remembered memes, I'm thinking of a guy I met in Newtown, Connecticut, who had a son in the first grade at Sandy Hook Elementary School when the shooting took place. His kid is alive—that should be said from the outset—but since the guy was teaching science at the middle school across town when the frantic texts and rumors and lockdown began, for a few hours he wasn't sure if his son had been shot. His son is alive because the shooter chose to step into a different classroom, but at first no one knew what had happened, including the guy's wife as she drove to the school to build gingerbread houses and saw an empty car blocking the road. By then, she could smell gunpowder searing the air. By then, there were sirens in the distance and soon a police officer held the gathered parents back as a group of children came running, one of whom was covered in blood and said, as she reached for her mom there in the crowd, *I'm alright, but the other kids are dead.* All of which is one reason why, when the emails and online postings began claiming that there had never been a shooting, that all of these parents were lying, that the grief of Sandy Hook was being performed, the guy's wife felt compelled to respond, to say what happened had happened. I was there, she wrote back, I was there. But the voices continued, a chorus that wouldn't stop calling the guy's wife *liar, conspirator,* no matter what facts she gave. When the threats began—*I'm bad for people's health,* someone wrote on Instagram. *Wait until I find your children*—the guy and his wife went to the police who told them there was nothing they could do. Passwords were changed, users were blocked: the taunts continued. After she wrote *This stalking needs to stop,* someone responded by posting a picture of their son accompanied by the words *This is stalking, bitch.* Which is when the guy renewed his permit to carry a gun and began slipping his .45 into its holster whenever he left the house. Perhaps you think you know where this is going. Perhaps this seems as predictable as any sloganeering phrase. Except this story refuses to be reduced to a single phrase. The guy kept his gun close, not knowing what else to do. Whenever he felt its heft—running errands, driving his car—maybe it seemed as if order could be restored, or maybe the gun made him feel as if he could stop the worst thing from becoming still worse. One morning, the guy drove to the middle school where he'd been teaching for years and, running late for a meeting, stepped into the building with the gun holstered under his coat. Maybe he just wasn't thinking. Maybe it was carelessness, arrogance, indifference to the rules. The guy knows that the word *mistake* doesn't cut it. Closer would be some word that doesn't exist for a fuck-up spilling out of desperation, or perhaps a desire to shield while also circumventing grief and trying to find some kind of foothold in the wake of twenty children being shot in his hometown. But the guy isn't interested in the words we might choose. Instead, he's thinking about the choices he should have made rather than strolling to the photocopier to prepare for class and watching the machine's light flare a few times across his hands as he pressed down on a book's spine before he was approached by the principal and asked to lift up his jacket. He knew then he'd be leaving in handcuffs. He didn't yet know that he'd lose his teaching license, or that the prosecutor's first offer would be a year in prison with a four-year suspended sentence. That without written permission he could never again pick up his son after school, or attend school events, or vote at a public school. That any future employer would see his mugshot online. That some of his friends in town would never speak to him again, and one day he'd find himself standing in a shaded corner of his yard, unemployed, listening to afternoon traffic push past, telling his story to some guy who, for whatever it's worth, didn't know what words to say.

Fake News Bus Stop Prayer

Although most mornings we only talk about whether it feels like
snow or just allow the silence to grow between us

while our kids whip the air with willow branches, making wide Z's
with three quick strokes, today Indigo's dad Pat was on a tear,

fired up after ABC News aired a report called *Slaughter in Syria*
& by mistake used footage from a Kentucky machine gun shoot,

an event, we learned, he attends every year in order to unleash
full-automatic fire into dishwashers rigged with propane tanks.

There are things to say, all of them better than what I managed
in the moment, which was a few muttered words intended

to derail his fake news rant & pull those of us gathered at the end
of Orchard Drive back from the brink of needing to respond

to rage we didn't share. Neighbor Pat, from within the absolute
silence of this page, I'll confess that I hope to never again hear you

describe what it's like to spray bullets into refrigerators, speed boats,
barrels of fuel. And yet, who am I to pretend to know nothing

of the pleasure of ruin, especially after the Tri-County Fair,
where I forked over a few extra bucks in order for my family to watch

the school bus smash-up derby, where my sticky blue wristband
proclaimed *yes* to wreckage, to wincing & mock groans, *yes*

to a hymn of broken glass where the point was good riddance
& to see our look-both-ways world shattered, to stalk & batter

& T-bone some chump, then back up & floor it again? To bellow
Yeah, baby! as my Oliver did, cheering even louder

when the #19 caught fire, the flames lapping across its hood,
making the air horn blare its mournful time-out cry

so that the firemen could trudge in from the sidelines
without much urgency, as if phoning it in, as if saying

this shit happens all the time. See? Pat, whom I barely know,
whom I've twice seen wearing a *Gun Control Means*

Using Both Hands T-shirt, I could do better by you.
If I wanted to rummage for some paltry common ground,

I'm guessing we could both agree too much shit happens
all the time, that our sidelines are empty of anyone

ready to step in, & that another form of fake news is pretending
you are the you in a poem you'll never read. This morning,

post–bus stop drop off, it's worth remembering we both hate
that guy who once gunned his Beamer past the school bus

& if neither of us believe prayer or poetry or any other word
for casting words into silence is sufficient to keep us safe,

maybe we could admit we share more than weather,
wreckage, daily farewells. Each afternoon, we stand together

on one scrappy length of grass until the bus returns
at 3:25 on the dot & that one kid in the backseat either mimes

little pistol shots at my face or flaps her little wrists in a gesture
of goodbye mixed with an attempt at flight as Laurie the driver

unfolds her sign, flashing her all's-well thumbs-up that means
not just *have-at-it*, but *go stumble-racing, backpacks jostling,*

across the asphalt in madcap joy-relief. Neighbor Pat, I know
I'll never share any of this with you, but for what it's worth

today, I swear, I want to intone at least half of the two-line
benediction I found on the machine gun range's website

thanks to you. It begins *The shoot takes place rain or shine*
& ends *The Good Lord willing, the creek doesn't rise.*

Poem Not Ending with Blossoms

Think of an oar, the cop said, & I pictured one
                                     raised & dripping
above the waves, *how it'll slice through water or, if you turn it,*

it'll slam against the surface instead, the metaphor intended
to explain the difference between hollow point & round nose

bullets, although the more
                             I imagined the gripped oar, its dip
or clumsy splash, the further I seemed to drift from the work

of any gun, yet without ever gliding
                                  from here, this once-
bustling, fluorescent-lit, seventh-floor space that used to be

Police Headquarters but had been gutted after a recent move
which left behind only a few detectives to wade through decades

of rape kits & FedEx boxes of narcotics in a storehouse maze
that ended in what had once been
                               a communal shower, now crowded

with trash bags stuffed with heroin & guarded by a display
of horror hostess Elvira adorned with a respirator mask. He offered

another comparison—*it's a choice between*
                               an ice pick or hammer
passing through your chest—cued perhaps by the Property Room

we'd toured upstairs, a place where everything linked
to a violent crime was grouped
                         by semblance in untidy heaps:

toasters crowding shelves next to microwaves, laptops stacked
near rows of flat-screen TVs, & sledgehammers tossed

on a cord-tangled mess
                        of nail guns & drills. There were guns,
of course—more than forty thousand, piled into filing cabinets,

shopping carts, or rain barrels, depending on their size. *Over here—*
he pointed to a mannequin head perched on six prosthetic limbs—

we're trying to make a full body,
                        but only have one head & these legs.
Why, I asked—since it seemed worth asking—are there so many

baby swings in here? *Sometimes,*
                        you don't want to know. But
because I'd wanted to know how a bullet works for reasons

I can no longer explain,
                        he led me downstairs to Bertha,
a test-fire tank made from Plexiglas, pool liners, & iron beams.

The name just suits her. She's sturdy, reliable, & takes bullets
all day without complaint. Industrial gray, with a tiny flag

tucked between her exhaust fan & switch, Bertha reminded me
of something
                        from the off-limits corner of shop class where

instead of building birdhouses, we spent our time folding
sheets of metal until they became
                        blade-like things we loved

to hold, wield, jab, content to wound
                        nothing but air. And how
did it feel to test-fire thousands of guns each year? *Boring,*

he said. *You end up*

          deaf & stuck with a bunch of water
too polluted to dump. Then he loaded two hollow points,

slipped his Glock into Bertha's PVC pipe,

          called out *Ears for two!*
& fired both rounds. The sound of gunshots was chased

by the metallic chime of cartridges dropping to the floor,
a slow slosh of water, one screw rolling in half circles

across the tank's trapdoor. Call that an American song
& nothing happens

          or worse. Although perhaps it's worse

to admit that after he netted the metal nubs & placed them
into my hand, their split tips

          curling back in petal-like shapes

extending from a center copper speck, *blossom* was the word
that came to mind. Even if,

          months later, I saw some earrings online

made from the same kind of bullets, each one flower-shaped
& described by the artist as *clear coated & tumbled*

to a smooth finish, that doesn't change how much I'd wished
for a different word to hold

          in that cramped room as little waves

moved, then stopped. It's possible

          the figurative ran its course
here a while back. Do we really need a personified tank

& metaphor of an oar smacking the surface
                                    of a lake where
they pour Bertha's lead-tainted water each week to understand

we're paddling nowhere? Once, the cop told me, they received
a call about someone bleeding on a bus. They pulled the vehicle over

& found a guy using a broken-off tree branch
                                    to gouge a bullet
from his calf. I'm still trying to picture this, still trying to form

the image of the man & the branch
                            he held. It was November.
Nothing was blooming in Cleveland once again when he told them

hell yes, he'd been shot, a few blocks back. Fuck off, kindly
leave him alone, & he'd just get the hell on with his day.

The Etymology of Gazebo

Tamir Rice (2002–2014)

will always have a hole in it

filled with guesswork
year after year. Most claim

it appeared without warning—
taking the ending of a future

tense for gaze that collided

with a verb shaped by a pronoun
which gives rise to *I shall see*

or perhaps *I will look*,
both phrases suggesting

a promise still to come—yet
the idea contains a void

you have to pretend isn't there.
Break open the roots & you'll need

to choose whether to believe
in a prefix that hints at

the way we see & an ending
that offers the image of a gazebo

being pulled apart piece by piece

as it's packed up & moved to a city
where it'll be built all over again.

People are tending to it with care,
shoveling dirt, carrying lengths

of metal & wood, scraping
shingles from the roof,

disassembling everything

down to the ribbons knotting
the beams, down to the cement

picnic table strapped to a chain
& hovering a few feet above

the ground while a vehicle
somewhere loudly proclaims

it's moving backward
again. Back up here

just a bit & you may want to ask
if it's safe to assume whenever

we sit beneath a structure
open on all sides that provides

shelter from the sun & rain, our hope
is to look, to see. We might not have

any interest in seeing what's right
in front of us, much like the man who,

before he strolled off & called the police,
sat in the gazebo just a few feet away,

silently watching but not seeing

a twelve-year old kid holding
a toy gun. Is there space here

for another theory? Some believe
we inherited the word through

words no one now speaks that mean
honor & heed, although those roots,

looking at them now, seem
like clusters of letters that say

nothing at all. Our words continue

to fail & yet here I sit, peering into
the name of some meager thing,

unable to stop pulling it apart,

as if that offered a kind of prayer
instead of a means to avert my gaze

from another child dead too soon.

After the gazebo was moved—
so that it would not be destroyed,

so that there might still be a place
to reflect & remember

& this death might not be

so easy to forget—the man who preserved it
wanted to remind us that words

like *memorial & honor* so often slip
through our hands like water, water

that becomes a trampled stretch of snow

which lingers in a park through
the end of November wherever

the gazebo's shadow falls.

Online, you can see Tamir Rice
on the security camera, moments

before he's shot, scoop a bit of snow

from the grass & shape it into a ball
with one hand before walking a few steps

& tossing it with a little arc
onto the sidewalk where it stays

a little while more.

The Dug-Up Gun Museum

Unearthed from homesteads or Deadwood dirt,
       shoveled up in Tombstone, Nebraska, Vermont, from the muck
    of the Missouri's banks or burned-out cabins,
from a goat barn, ghost towns, gold country, battlefields,
       this one discovered in the crotch of an oak,
    this one pulled loaded from a riverbed

with mother-of-pearl handle still attached: case after case
       of rifles & pistols, all battered, mottled,
    rippling with rust & now nestled in vitrines
on piles of carted-in dirt, rocks, & tufts of grass
       in order, I imagine, to help us imagine
    the places from which they came. Or *to keep us from thinking*

about guns as things
       no one ever touched, the owner told me, which meant noticing,
    for instance, one had misfired
before someone hammered the cylinder back into place,
       or a shotgun's stock pierced with a bullet hole,
or how once-held pistol grips had rotted away, leaving behind

steel frames, each one curved like a letter from an alphabet
       we almost recognize or, given the earth's slow erasure of things,
    like a word being taken back. *It's all about history*
coming alive, he said, although wasn't history already
       alive, on the move, everywhere
    around us? Just up the road, at the Cody Firearms Experience,

you can pull the trigger
       on every American gun, pour powder down the barrel
    of a pioneer musket, or batter your shoulder
with an M-16. Their slogan: *From Flintlock*
       to Full Auto, an alliterative phrase that glides through
    three centuries of weapons that shaped our country—

Winchester, Gatling, Tommy gun, breechloading trapdoor. Even if
  there's more to say about euphemism lathing
 the edges of the verb *shape*,
here instead was a woman wearing a plastic sheriff's badge
  & showing me a cardboard target
 with a black & white photo of a man. On one side,

he glowered & pointed a pistol. On the other, his hands were raised
  with the gun tucked into his jeans. *This is a typical good-guy-*
 bad-guy course, she told me, a bit bored
as she clamped the target into place
  & entered a code that made the man jerk back
 then turn to one side so that we could only see the target's edge

soaring down the lane until
  it paused for a moment, then flipped to reveal
 the man pointing the gun. On it went, the man spinning & flung
back & forth, ready to shoot
  then raising his hands or—sometimes with a full-turn flick—ready
 to shoot again. Then the lights shut off

& there was the sound of the man sliding down the lane
  just before a double burst of light broke the darkness above
 the good guy, who rotated to become the guy
holding the gun & everything
  went dark again. You get the idea. The plan was to prepare
 teachers to carry guns in schools, although of course

there would be much more. Picture a classroom
  staged with toppled desks
 & students pretending to be wounded or dead
as the math teacher bursts through the door
  with his prop gun, in an instant needing to assess, choose, aim,
 his finger on the trigger just like the life-size John Wayne

out in the lobby, at ease yet ready
  for whatever might come. This was the same *Rio Bravo*

cardboard figure, I learned, used by the high school
during active shooter drills, when the two principals would carry
       the Duke along with Clint Eastwood
from *The Good, the Bad, & the Ugly* through the school

in order to represent two gunmen on the loose, prowling
       classrooms, offices, the gym,
   seeking out stragglers, floating down the hallway
the way the real John Wayne, in town to promote *The Shootist*,
       once glided down main street beside a thirty-foot Winchester
   in a Fourth of July parade. You can still see the prop mounted

on a gun shop's roof. Although if locals describe actor & rifle cruising
       the road side by side, the gun offering
   the legend a place to sometimes lean
as the procession crept forward, in every photograph I've seen
       of that day, Wayne grins from the back of a Cadillac
   & there's no oversized gun in sight, meaning

even the basic facts are wrong
       & the Duke either trailed the Winchester, following it slowly
   through the heat as the crowd hooted above the drums
or the dark two-foot O
       of its barrel tracked him from behind
   as he drifted up the street. For some reason,

this seems to matter. For some reason,
       I keep thinking of workers unbolting the gun
   from the parade float, then using a crane to lift it
to that rooftop, guiding it into place, aiming it south, tending to it,
       mending things whenever the sky broke
   through, making sure the gun would hover above

forevermore. Patched, reinforced, secured,
       it's not going anywhere now & now
   will always cast its shadow down
on the street where they stage a shoot-out in the summer
       six nights a week when it's all about the standoff
   & showdown, the quick draw & sudden bang

followed by the crowd's cheers. Does the storyline matter? Not long
        after a preamble in which Cody Custer praises
    the killer crab puffs at a restaurant a few blocks away,
Wyatt Earp & Doc Holliday pinch-hit for an AWOL sheriff, shooting down
        the bad guys outside of a wheeled-in saloon. The point is
    nothing stays holstered & no one imagines

bullets entering flesh. We want to see
        bodies fall & hands flutter at the hammer
    like they're supposed to. And we want it all
to end with applause rather than what happened a few summers back,
        when one of the guys loaded his gun
    with live rounds by mistake & shot a few tourists

& some kayaks for rent across the street. Now, of course,
        everyone checks their weapons
    more than once & the group, for insurance purposes,
changed their name from the Gunfighters to the Wild Bunch,
        even if it's all the same show with the same
    Butch Cassidy in borrowed chaps making jokes

about *biting the bullet*, a metaphor we use for any hardship,
        meaning it drifted free
    from meaning long ago & refuses
to claim anything about actual bullets slipped into
        the mouth as a source of meager reprieve, unlike
the chewed up, pockmarked metal nubs, now barely bullets at all,

lined up along a shelf at the Dug-Up Gun Museum, dug up
        from who knows where. There must be something more to say
    about bullets as a source of pain
as well as pain's insufficient cure,
        but instead I'm turning to the five-year-old in Pittsburgh
    who found a pistol on his playground at school,

not buried at all but just tossed there in the grass
        where the little O of its barrel glinted & summoned him

from the swings. He picked it up & fired a bullet
& yet for what it's worth no one was shot that day. Isn't that the best
         we can hope for, given that
no one's asking *if* anymore & the guns are in our grass,

our schools, our dirt & we know
         there are still more to find, or given no one's thinking about how
         Chekhov wrote *One must never place a loaded rifle on stage*
if it doesn't ever go off. It's wrong to make promises
         you don't keep. Even if America buried
many of its promises long ago, when it comes to the gun

& bullets we refuse to fail. *O say*
         can you see, we sing all the time, as if this were a question
we wanted to ask although no one's really asking
what you might have seen
         since the words that follow never change: another dawn,
         another bomb-burst, all that stuff about the flag. The word for that O,

if it matters, is apostrophe, which means literally
         to turn away in the sense of leaning in & calling out & from there
following whatever words come, which is all
I might have hoped for when I crouched down in the museum
         for a last look & the owner of the museum paused too
         & together we peered into a space we'd both already seen

filled with nothing but rocks & a scribble of grass & guns
         & we looked once more at the rusted, lopsided O
of one barrel's dark tip that signified nothing in itself but we tried
to imagine for a moment whatever else
         we could beyond the gun & then what next O

given how her eyes lift toward something beyond

the frame & the way a veil plumes her face like smoke,

inflaming you, inspiring you to steal the keepsake photo

from your friend in a joke that's not a joke, allowing

the seeds of your obsession to flourish? Maybe with

enough rain & sun those seeds will grow into more

cotton someone will need to pick. Or perhaps they'll

take root not in the fields but along a coast that can't be

far from the place Lincoln dreamed & wrote about

hours before he died: *an indescribable vessel that was*

moving with great rapidity toward a dark & indefinite shore.

Portrait of America as exactly that. Portrait of America

as you-name-it ticking forward, rehashed, brought back

once more like Lillian Gish returned to Ford's theater

decades later, cast now as the aggrieved widow-to-be

in the mediocre made-for-TV movie *The Day Lincoln Died*,

where the same trigger-squeeze makes her become

a punchline we've already heard: *Other than that,*

Mrs. Lincoln, how did you like the play? Portrait of America

as a joke about dying that will never die, as yet another

aftermath's *other-than-that, other-than-that* refrain.

Notes

Some of the content included in "Portrait of America as a Friday the 13th Flashlight Tour of the Winchester Mystery House" originally appeared in my libretto for *Inheritance*, a chamber opera developed collaboratively with artist Ligia Bouton, director Cara Consilvio, composer Lei Liang, and soprano Susan Narucki. Sarah Winchester, heiress to the Winchester Repeating Arms Company, built her labyrinth-like home in San Jose, California, where it is now promoted as one of America's "most haunted places." The quoted phrase reproduced in the stained glass window is from Shakespeare's *Troilus and Cressida*. This poem is dedicated to Lei Liang.

"The Wrong Question More Than Once" quotes a Philadelphia trauma surgeon who was interviewed for the article "What Bullets Do To Bodies," written by Jason Fagone and published in *Highline Magazine*. The italicized lines in the poem's second half are taken from an interview I conducted with Pamela Montgomery-Bosley, co-founder of Purpose Over Pain, an organization that advocates for common-sense changes to America's gun laws and offers support to parents who have lost children to gun violence. This poem is dedicated to Pamela Montgomery-Bosley.

"Here the Thing with Feathers Isn't Hope" owes a debt to Emily Dickinson's poem "'Hope' is the Thing with Feathers." The sculpture at the center of this poem—"Conversation Piece"—was created by Chicago-based artist Garland Martin Taylor, who told me the story of his artwork's road trip through America. This poem is dedicated to Garland Martin Taylor.

"D-Day: Albrightsville, Pennsylvania" contains details from my visit to Skirmish Paintball's annual "Invasion of Normandy" event.

"Land of 1000 Dances" references several versions of that song, including Chris Kenner's original recording, the subsequent cover hit by Cannibal and the Headhunters, and Patti Smith's title track from her 1975 album *Horses*, which incorporates lyrics from "Land of 1000 Dances." The Colt Firearms Collection is housed in the Museum of Connecticut History.

"Portrait of America as the Hands of Peter Graves in *The Night of the Hunter*" contains a few lines of dialogue taken from Charles Laughton's haunting 1955 film, *The Night of the Hunter*. The poem also references the 2013 police shooting of Wayne Jones in Martinsburg, West Virginia. Jones, a schizophrenic man experiencing homelessness, was fatally shot twenty-two times by five police officers after being initially approached for not walking on the sidewalk.

"Jack Ruby's .38 Colt Cobra" includes details gathered from online information about the infamous gun and from my own interview with Anthony V. Pugliese III.

The narrative and details included in "Operation Lion Claws: Fort Hood, Texas" are a compressed version of events that took place during a weekend-long military simulation. Although numerous American companies offer similar experiences, I was specifically interested in learning more about airsoft battle simulations hosted on federal military bases. Robert E. Lee is believed to have spoken his words about the seductive nature of war following the Battle of Fredericksburg.

"Green Means Literally a Thousand Things or More" incorporates some phrases and images from Dylan Thomas's poem "Fern Hill."

"Mass Shootings Are Actually Pretty Rare, but Here's What to Do If You're Ever in One" borrows its title from an article that appeared in *Self Magazine*. The poem is modeled on Wisława Szymborska's poem "Every Case," as translated by Grażyna Drabik and Sharon Olds.

"Guy with a Gun" draws upon several interviews I conducted with Newtown, Connecticut residents Geri and Jason Adams. This poem is dedicated to Jason Adams.

"Poem Not Ending with Blossoms" is dedicated to Todd and Diane Marazzi.

Two years after Tamir Rice was killed by a police officer, the city of Cleveland planned to destroy the gazebo that marked the site of the twelve-year-old's death. Thanks to the efforts of Rice's mother Samaria Rice and the Rebuild Foundation, a nonprofit founded by artist Theaster Gates, the gazebo was instead dismantled and moved to the Stony Island Arts Bank in Chicago. "The Etymology of *Gazebo*" references this act of preservation and paraphrases remarks made by Gates during the dedication ceremony. "Today, I hope you will join me in reflecting on Tamir and honoring Tamir's mom as she honors her son," Gates said, before raising questions about assigning a name to the work they had done. "Then there are these other words, like 'memorial' and 'honor' and 'commemoration.' None of them seem exactly right. When Samaria called, there was some work to do. This site of trauma needed a home. In the name of Tamir and in the name of beauty, we can use this now sacred space to have some Black joy and be critical, radical and disruptive. Mourn and celebrate."

"The Dug-Up Gun Museum" contains details borrowed from the real-life Dug Up Gun Museum, located in Cody, Wyoming. I'm grateful to Hans Kurth, the museum's co-owner and curator, for giving me a guided tour of his firearms collection during my visit to Cody.

"Portrait of America as a Philadelphia Derringer Abraham Lincoln Assasination Box Set Replica" references D.W. Griffith's racist 1915 film *Birth of a Nation* (originally called *The Clansman*). It also references a dream Abraham Lincoln had the night before he was killed. Lincoln shared the dream during his last cabinet meeting, and it was subsequently described by his Secretary of the Navy, Gideon Welles.

Acknowledgments

Some of these poems, sometimes in slightly altered versions, previously appeared in the following publications:

The Academy of American Poets' Poem-a-Day: "Green Means Literally a Thousand Things or More";

AGNI: (as "A Brief History of Bang") "D-Day: Albrightsville, Pennsylvania," "Operation Lion Claws: Fort Hood, Texas";

American Poetry Review: "Portrait of America as a Friday the 13th Flashlight Tour of the Winchester Mystery House," "The Dug-Up Gun Museum";

Brevity: "Jack Ruby's .38 Colt Cobra," "Solipsism: A Story";

The Common: "Guy with a Gun," "Portrait of America as a Philadelphia Derringer Abraham Lincoln Assassination Box Set Replica";

Copper Nickel: "Poem Not Ending with Blossoms";

Five Points: "Land of 1000 Dances";

Massachusetts Review: "Mass Shootings Are Actually Pretty Rare, but Here's What to Do If You're Ever in One," "Planet Fitness," "Shooting Justin Bieber & bin Laden in the Woods";

New England Review: "Here the Thing with Feathers Isn't Hope," "The Wrong Question More Than Once";

On the Seawall: "Fake News Bus Stop Prayer";

Southern Humanities Review: "The Etymology of *Gazebo*";

Zócalo Public Square: "Thousands or Millions of Tiny Dots of Varying Size."

This book is deeply indebted to the care and generosity of many people, without whom these poems would not have been possible.

Huge thanks to the editors of the journals in which many of these pieces previously appeared.

To Creative Capital, which provided invaluable support for both the creation and staging of *Inheritance*, a collaborative chamber opera based on the life of Sarah Winchester.

To Courtney Hodell and Michael Taeckens from the Whiting Foundation for all of their guidance and insights. To the Whiting Foundation, for their extraordinary support.

To Paisley Rekdal, who selected "The Etymology of Gazebo" as the winner of the 2020 Auburn Witness Poetry Prize from the *Southern Humanities Review*.

To Jessica Skwire Routhier, for her eagle eye and meticulous edits.

To the Murato-Long clan, who kick-started my thinking about America's proxy guns by hosting a paintball birthday celebration for ten-year-old Ren.

Deep gratitude to Jason Adams, Pamela Bosley, Krista Hanley, and Peter Munro, who humbled me with their willingness to share their experiences.

When I first began traveling around America and speaking to people about guns, I had little idea what shape this book would ultimately take. I'm extremely grateful for the time, expertise, and patience of numerous people, whose words and stories both directly and indirectly informed every one of these pages. In Chicago, enormous thanks to: Halleh Akbarnia, Tom Vanden Berk and Derrick K. Baker from UCAN, Susan Johnson from Chicago Survivors, and artist Garland Martin Taylor. In Cleveland, to Detective Todd Marazzi. In Cody, to Yancy Bonner, Paul Brock, Patrick Coutre, Sarah Growney, Mayor Matt Hall, Elizabeth Hansen, Hans Kurth, Ashley Hlebinsky, Jerimiah Johnston, Tom Keegan, Ken Martin, Sheriff Scott Steward, Scott Weber, and Ben Werner. Additional thanks to Mike Capps, Chris Cheng, Genghis Cohen, Coxy, Launa Cramer, Garrett Ferguson, Ryan Lawrence, Diane Marazzi, Edgardo Padin, Anthony Pugliese, Senator Al Simpson, Philip Smith, Piper Smith, and Spooky.

And I will be forever grateful to the people of Newtown, Connecticut—especially Geri Adams, Jason Adams, Tom Campbell, Patricia Llodra, Brian Mauriello, and Father Robert Weiss—who were willing to speak with me and share their grief.

For their friendship, encouragement, and insights, all of which shaped these poems in innumerable ways, thanks to Ciaran Berry, Ryan Black, Chad Davidson, Jenny George, Kathleen Graber, Dana Levin, Nathan McClain, Patrick Phillips, and Tom Sleigh.

To the entire fabulous BOA staff—especially Peter Conners, Michelle Dashevsky, and Gena Hartman, and—for their incredible care in bringing this book forth into the world.

To Sandy Knight for her stunning cover design.

To Nick Cave, for his generous permission to reproduce a detail from *Until*, his magisterial 2016 installation at MASS MoCA.

To my sons, Oliver and Cyrus, who not only weathered my travels as I was writing this book, but were waiting for me back home with questions and joy.

To my parents, for all of their love and support.

And, always, to Ligia Bouton, who guarded my far-flung solitude, who was the first reader of every word here, and who somehow never wavered, despite this project's many veers.

About the Author

Matt Donovan is the author of two previous collections of poetry: *Rapture & the Big Bam* (Tupelo Press) and *Vellum* (Mariner), as well as a book of lyric essays, *A Cloud of Unusual Size and Shape: Meditations on Ruin and Redemption* (Trinity University Press). Donovan's work has been published in numerous literary journals, including *AGNI, American Poetry Review, The Believer, Gettysburg Review, Kenyon Review, Poetry, Seneca Review, Threepenny Review,* and *Virginia Quarterly Review*. Donovan is the recipient of a Whiting Award, a Rome Prize in Literature, a Pushcart Prize, the Levis Reading Prize, and an NEA Fellowship in Literature. In 2017, he received a Creative Capital Grant for *Inheritance*, a collaborative multimedia chamber opera based on the life of Sarah Winchester. Donovan serves as Director of the Boutelle-Day Poetry Center at Smith College.

BOA Editions, Ltd. American Poets Continuum Series

Colophon

BOA Editions, Ltd., a not-for-profit publisher of poetry and other literary works, fosters readership and appreciation of contemporary literature. By identifying, cultivating, and publishing both new and established poets and selecting authors of unique literary talent, BOA brings high-quality literature to the public.

Support for this effort comes from the sale of its publications, grant funding, and private donations.

The publication of this book is made possible, in part, by the special support of the following individuals:

Anonymous (x2)
Angela Bonazinga & Catherine Lewis
Jennifer Cathy, *in memory of Angelina Guggino*
Chris Dahl, *in memory of Sandy McClatchy*
David J. Fraher, *in memory of Al Poulin*
Bonnie Garner
James Long Hale
Margaret Heminway
Sandi Henschel, *in memory of Anthony Piccione*
Kathleen Holcombe
Teresa D. Johnson
Nora A. Jones
Paul LeFerriere & Dorrie Parini
John & Barbara Lovenheim
Richard Margolis & Sherry Phillips
Frances Marx
Joe McElveney
Dan Meyers, *in honor of J. Shepard Skiff*
Boo Poulin
Jim Robie & Edith Matthai, *in memory of Peter Hursh*
Deborah Ronnen
William Waddell & Linda Rubel
Michael Waters & Mihaela Moscaliuc